AMERICAN ESSAYS IN LITURGY

SERIES EDITOR, EDWARD FOLEY

LAY PRESIDING
THE ART OF LEADING PRAYER

KATHLEEN HUGHES, R.S.C.J.

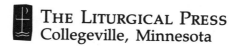
THE LITURGICAL PRESS
Collegeville, Minnesota

Cover design by Mark Coyle.

CONTENTS

SURFACING THE ISSUES

More than ten years ago Robert Hovda published *Strong, Loving and Wise,* a splendid work on the art of liturgical presidency. Hovda developed his model of presidency and the role of the presider in planning, preparation, environment, presence, and style on the foundation of a solid theology of ministry. He emphasized worship as an integral event with particular rhythms and patterns. He presented the relational nature of the presider's role and communicated the basic principles of ritual activity rather than simply techniques. This book became an ideal manual for those classes and workshops devoted to presiding. The author specified his intended audience in his introduction:

> The Liturgical Conference publishes this book with theological schools and seminaries in mind, bishops, priests, pastors, deacons, any others who regularly preside in public worship, and those responsible for continuing education programs for clergy. Its intent is to serve both those who preside in liturgy and those who are training for offices which will involve such presidency.[1]

Hovda's book has been widely acclaimed and has proven most useful precisely in the schools and seminaries which he hoped to reach. One sign of the success of this work is the fact that it is now in a fifth edition. It has served as inspiration for a generation of the community's newly ordained and motivated countless veteran presiders in the process of "retooling."

Why, then, another book on presiding?

The simplest response may be to suggest that the unique strength of *Strong, Loving and Wise* has proven more recently to be a limitation, namely, that the book does not directly address the specific situation, questions, or concerns of the growing number of non-ordained women and men asked to lead others in prayer. This is a new situation for the Church, prompted in part by an increasing clergy shortage, but prompted as well by the discovery of the gift of leadership of prayer among ever-widening circles of ministry and care.

Side by side with those persons being trained to preside at the Church's public worship, the liturgy strictly so-called, is another, larger band of women and men whose leadership is called forth in less-structured, less-patterned moments. Side by side are men preparing to assume leadership of the community's sacramental life, and men and women who, because of evident gift and grace, are being asked with greater frequency to lead assemblies and communities and families in prayers of praise and thanksgiving, of reconciliation and hope, sometimes with some preparation but more often spontaneously, on the spur of the moment. This monograph is for that wider band of Christian disciples, often reluctant leaders because they are untrained in any formal way in the art and the science of presiding—and perhaps even unwilling to give such a grandiloquent title to such a simple event.

The reflections which follow will be designed precisely for such "reluctant presiders," hesitant, perhaps, because of the power of traditional role distinctions, yet needing to acknowledge at some fundamental level that each of us *ought* to be able to be called upon in certain circumstances to lead others in prayer. The intended audience thus includes parents learning to bless their children, loved ones brought to deepest prayer at a sick bed, unsuspecting group participants who are asked to open a meeting with prayer, dinner guests invited to bless God at table, family or friends longing to be able to comfort one another at a wake service or a funeral, parishioners asked to preside at a Lenten evening prayer, and sponsors initiating their catechumens into the ways of Christian prayer.

The opportunities for Christian men and women to exercise "presidency" of the "assembly" are endless. Despite such opportunities, however, we carefully train our liturgical presiders and demand developed competency in what, for better or for worse, has come to be called "presidential style," while opportunities for training of lay presiders are nearly non-existent, and resources appear to be limited and scattered.

Why another book?

There is another reason for a fresh reflection on the leadership of prayer specifically addressed to the lay leader. We need to explore lay presiding not simply because circumstances have forced us to admit new members to the "presidential" ranks, but because these new members are asking new questions and urging new attitudes.

Lay presiders bring a new set of questions, some of them raised by Christian feminists looking for new ways of praying. Such questions concern the nature of leadership itself as well as appropriate gesture, language, garb and arrangement of space. Lay presiders prompt a new look at the way we structure our prayer, the way we appropriate the traditional symbols, and the way we acknowledge the presence of the Holy One in our midst. These questions must be taken seriously and allowed to challenge our habitual ways of relating within the assembly both to one another and to the Lord of our lives. The exploration of these questions may shed light on sacramental patterns of prayer as well.

The questions lay presiders might wish to explore are also prompted by the often amorphous nature of the task itself. While the community's ordained members generally preside at highly structured patterns of prayer for which resources are readily available complete with rubrical directives, the very fluidity and flexibility of "unofficial" patterns of prayer are both daunting and threatening. How does one structure a simple prayer? Are there any rules or guidelines? Where do we find helpful resources? How do we develop sufficient confidence in our own authority, creativity and skill so that it would be possible to improvise a prayer or offer a blessing with ease?

Quite apart from the disinclination of the official Church

to recognize the presence of lay presiders within its ranks and to offer adequate training and resources for these women and men to assume their ministry, it is my belief that two other factors have stunted the development of lay leadership, both of which are concerned with the "vesting of authority" for the leadership of prayer.

In some measure, and perhaps only subconsciously, lay members of the assembly have not given one another permission to lead prayer—or have given it grudgingly. Furthermore, quite apart from the authority others may offer, few lay women and men have given themselves permission to preside. The nature of this authority necessary to assume the leadership of prayer is the first issue we shall address, because it will provide the foundation for the subsequent development of such issues as creativity and skill.

Consider the following vignette as illustrative of the role that "expectations" and "permissions" play in assuming the leadership of the community's prayer:

A good many years ago I attended the wake of a family friend. As I entered the funeral parlor, several persons converged in my direction. The parish priest had not arrived and the guests were becoming restless. Would I mind leading the rosary?

It was quite clear that hierarchical leadership patterns had unconsciously been adopted by the family. The parish priest was not available. Apparently the next best choice was a woman religious. Their choice seemed to suggest that "professional" religious are automatically better "pray-ers" than others, have more training in public prayer, possess the right "authority" to assume such leadership, or at least *ought* to be able to assume public leadership as part of their job description.

Furthermore, as was clear to me from the continuing anxious glances in the direction of the door, if Father arrived in the next few minutes, Sister's leadership mandate would be withdrawn. From the point of view of the family and their friends, I was offered their implicit blessing as a leader of prayer, and at that moment clearly vested with authority to preside, though a second choice in the order of their expectations.

Besides those of the family, another set of assumptions and expectations was operative that evening, namely, my own. While lay Catholics might presume that men and women religious know something about leading prayer, I was quite aware that "this woman religious" became instantly paralyzed. I, too, had always relied upon the ordained priest to provide all the necessary public rituals. I had no training in this area, and certainly had no special mystical relationship to God. In short, there was nothing to commend me as community leader of prayer except some misplaced trust on the part of my friends in "the grace of my vocation."

That experience is indelibly etched in my memory. Terror was my overriding response, carefully masked by a nod of the head and a weak smile, and I quite forgot anything I had ever observed of such rituals at the numerous wakes I had attended, even the mysteries of the Rosary! Whether joyful or sorrowful I do not know—but I do know that one of the "mysteries" which I announced for our meditation that evening was the Circumcision!

This vignette exemplifies so many unresolved questions and issues concerning the leadership of the community's prayer. First of all, it speaks of a time in the not-too-distant past when we turned to our parish priests to serve *all* of our ritual prayer needs, whether liturgical or devotional. We even deferred to ordained guests within our family homes and invited them to "say the grace" at our tables. The possibility, indeed the eminent suitability, for us ordinary folk to exercise leadership in situations of communal prayer has only slowly dawned on us in these years since Vatican II.

My own inability to assume a leadership role with ease, despite the fact that I had participated countless times in such services illustrates a second problem, a problem borne out again and again for me as I observe the level of readiness of my students at the beginning of a worship practicum. What has become abundantly clear is this: the men who come into the worship practicum who are ordination candidates have, perhaps for as long as they can remember, subconsciously appropriated the words and gestures, the structures and styles of celebration which

5

they have observed. They have *imagined* themselves in the role of presider and have appropriated what we might call "presidential" behavior. While these ordination candidates might need a great deal of practice and critique before becoming competent leaders of public prayer, they nevertheless have the advantage of years of active, imaginative participation as leaders of a community gathered for prayer. They have projected themselves, in their imagination, into the role of presider and have subconsciously appropriated that role.

Not so for potential *lay* leaders of prayer. Such persons, most often but not exclusively women, do not have that advantage. Our symbolic perceptions as well as our carefully delineated roles in the assembly have kept us outside of the sanctuary both literally and metaphorically. Lay men and women have not been given permission, either by the tradition, the community, or themselves, to imagine themselves in the role of presider. It is as simple as that. Thus, lay persons are at a clear disadvantage when beginning formal training as leaders of prayer. They have neither imagined themselves in particular roles nor become sensitized at some deep level about the patterns and structures of different forms of communal prayer. On the contrary, they have been subject to a type of subconscious ritual taboo: neither able to assume ritual leadership nor even to be welcome in sacred space. Consequently, they have not learned leadership qualities and skills "by osmosis" as have their ordained counterparts, because of other sets of expectations and because of permissions withheld—both of which nullified for them the possibility of creative projection.

It cannot be denied that for many, the person most influential in "denying permission" to be a leader of prayer has been the potential leader him or herself. Recently I attended a meeting of a Board of Trustees for which an agenda had circulated in advance. The first item was an opening prayer, assigned to the chairperson, a layman. He had known of this assignment prior to the meeting, yet he arrived unprepared and announced that he would be glad to "say" a prayer if someone would give him something to read.

Perhaps my friend did not know the simple structure of a "collect" style prayer. Perhaps he did not realize how many resources were available and how easy it would have been to find a prayer appropriate to the meeting and the Easter season which we were celebrating that week. Perhaps he did not believe himself capable of finding the right words to express our need for wit and wisdom in our deliberations that evening. In this instance a pattern had been established by the Board for each person in turn to open the meeting with a prayer, and thus each of us implicitly gave one another permission to lead the prayer. Beyond group expectations or permissions, however, we had in this situation an individual who had not given himself permission to be a leader of prayer—and his name is legion among clergy and laity alike.

We are in a new age of the Church's life. Perhaps prompted by a growing realization of the effects of the shortage of clergy—perhaps prompted, as well, by an understanding of the very nature of the Christian vocation, a new leadership is emerging in the community. Nevertheless, training competent leaders of the community's prayer remains a critical need in the contemporary Church.

There are many gifts; there are many ways to pray. Ordained and lay leadership of prayer are complementary in nature, both enriching the life and growth of the community of faith. Lay leadership of prayer may be regarded as a threat only by those who do not believe the Spirit in every age moves freely, offering gifts for the building up of the Church in faith and love.

A word of caution is in order as we begin. Lay leadership of Sunday worship, particularly in those communities where non-ordained members now preside at services of Word and/or Communion in the absence of ordained priests, has sometimes been regarded as a happy harbinger of the church of the future. I hope such is not the case! To believe that a community might be nourished on services of Word and Communion for long periods of time is to risk inevitably becoming a non-sacramental church. To suggest that priestless parishes are a hopeful development is madness! The community, as the title of one of Edward

7

Schillebeeckx' works suggests, has the *right* to a priest.[2] Until we are able to recognize and encourage in one another, man or woman, celibate or married, the gift and grace of leadership of the community's sacramental prayer we are caught in a situation where such abnormalities as Sunday Communion services will continue. That is a reality with which we are faced.

And yet we live in this in-between time. Women and men willing to lead the prayer of priestless communities in this interim period deserve our attention and all the assistance possible, that they may assume such ministry with grace and competence. The topic of Sunday assemblies at which lay persons preside will be addressed in these pages. But let us not, for a moment, regard these practices as anything but abnormal in our sacramental community.

A variety of different issues will occupy us in the pages which follow. We will examine some of the more theoretical questions which are now posed in the light of lay presidency of prayer as well as the attitudes, expectations and perceptions on the part of the community and the individual who would assume its leadership. A second set of issues and questions concerns the appropriation of the traditional patterns of prayer. Some of the words, the gestures, and the symbols of our tradition will be explored as well as the way these elements are joined in different configurations in differing situations. Finally, after a more theoretical discussion, and an exploration of traditional patterns of Christian prayer, particular qualities and skills of a leader of prayer will be examined.

This essay will therefore attempt to communicate some basic knowledge about the community's traditional patterns of prayer, about the symbols and gestures and words which have formed and transformed men and women over the ages. It will also address the very concrete skills needed by a leader of prayer. It will point to certain principles and some fundamental patterns of prayer and will suggest practical exercises which individuals and small groups might use to deepen their knowledge and love of the community's prayer and their authority in the exercise of its leadership.

And yet, it is important to acknowledge that none of us,

neither lay nor ordained, knows how to pray as we ought. Saint Paul urged us to recognize our utter dependence on the Spirit. Such humble recognition of our own weakness and limitation is the first and the most important quality of one who would lead the community in prayer.

BY WHOSE AUTHORITY

And when he entered the temple, the chief priests and the elders of the people came up to him as he was teaching, and said, *"By what authority are you doing these things, and who gave you this authority?"*

(Matt. 21:23)

By whose authority does one assume the leadership of the community's prayer, whether where two or three are gathered or in the larger assembly? What gives one the right to speak in the name of all? Are there ways in which, consciously or unconsciously, we empower or deny power to others in the exercise of their leadership, and for what reasons? Do we need the blessing of another or others before we are fit ministers of prayer?

Does authority come from the appropriation of knowledge of the Church's tradition? Absolutely. Is that enough? Surely not.

Does authority come from training and practice in the art of leadership? Absolutely, for such training allows one to be at ease and present to others, "un-self-conscious" in the best sense. Yet training and practice are not enough.

Does authority come from deputation, from some public ritual delegation of power to an individual with the consent of the community? Of course. Such is true of the present rite of ordination in which a community recognizes and blesses one or several members for the service of the community. That individual is granted, through orders, a juridical power within the community. Yet jurisdiction by itself is not enough, for the leadership we are examining finds its grounding not in credentials of power

11

but in the moral authority of striving for personal holiness. Is that not clear from the pages of the New Testament?

To sort out the meaning of authority it is enlightening to look at the variety of ways in which Jesus, bereft of "the power of jurisdiction," nevertheless was the subject of such extraordinary authority that friend and foe alike were forced to acknowledge that no one could compare with him. Though he was the son of a carpenter, though travelling with a simple ragtag band, though speaking in the language of story and parable rather than more erudite philosophical or theological categories, though rubbing shoulders with tax collectors and sitting down at table with sinners, though living an occasionally "Bohemian" life—having broken all the categories and shattered all the life-style idols set up by those who observed the *status quo*—nevertheless Jesus was recognized wherever he went as one "with authority," precisely in contrast to those who were the putative leaders of the community.

No one else spoke quite as he did: self-possessed, unself-conscious, never self-serving, not looking for a coterie of followers, pointing always beyond himself. There was something in his bearing, in his glance and smile, in the way he told the truth with love, tolerating all weakness excepting that of hypocrisy, which drew people to himself. There was something powerful and winning in his words of life and freedom. He spoke as one who knew human nature, who was no stranger to pain and doubt and fear, yet stood firm and unyielding. There was something believable and trustworthy about this man, something in his message which moved hearts and restored lives by reconciling and healing and making whole. There was something that made people pause and acknowledge, perhaps even despite themselves, that here was one who possessed authority.

And what of the source of Jesus' authority? Jesus would be the first to acknowledge that the authority which he possessed had its origin beyond himself. He did not speak or act on his own but on the authority of the One who sent him. Such authority was the gift of a contemplative outlook on the world: the fruit of his single-minded and single-hearted obedience to the One whom he called Abba.

In its simplest expression authority has to do with "authoring": with producing, creating, and bringing into being. It further implies the power or right so to act in relation to others or even to oneself. Jesus was one who possessed authority. The extent of his authority was visible in the life he communicated by his presence and his power. It is here, perhaps, that the chasm between jurisdiction and moral authority is most clearly delineated. For who can legislate the respect of others? What ritual can guarantee personal recognition simply in virtue of an office conferred? Who can demand the obedience of others except in virtue of personal authority?

To become a leader of the community's prayer is to pledge oneself to a way of life, outside the praying assembly, which allows Christ, *the* leader of prayer, to live and move and be in us. All of us are potential leaders of prayer because all of us have been plunged into Jesus' death for the life of the world through our baptism. All of us are potential leaders of prayer because we are members of the royal priesthood which we entered when we were initiated into this community of disciples. All of us are potential leaders of prayer to the extent that we acknowledge that it is Jesus, the Christ who lives on still to make intercession on our behalf. All of us are potential leaders of prayer insofar as we truly believe that *only* the Son makes known the One he called Abba.

Our leadership will have a ring of authenticity and truth insofar as we believe it is in the power of Jesus' abundant and life-giving Spirit that we are even able to say "Jesus is Lord." Participation in Jesus' life of obedience and recognition that Jesus is *the* leader of prayer are absolute prerequisites for one who aspires to serve the community as leader of prayer.

Does all of this suggest that only the handful of living saints among us or only those who have the same kind of extraordinary magnetism as did Christ have any right to lead prayer? On the contrary, it suggests 1) that in virtue of baptism *every* Christian as a member of the royal priesthood is a potential representative of this baptismal order; 2) that only Christ is leader of prayer and thus any individual, ordained or lay, needs to act in such a way as to enable the *transparent* presence of Christ in the midst of the community; 3) that such authority will be affirmed in those who, like Christ, bring others to life, and who allow the life we share to come to fullest articulation through their attentiveness to the presence of God in their lives. Such is to give some theological foundation to the question of prayer leadership with the authority that comes from Baptism as well as a pattern of faithful obedience to the life of the Spirit accepted in virtue of Baptism.

Before leaving the topic of authority, however, we yet need to raise the important issue of power and its potential abuse. In contemporary experience the word "power" often has a decidedly negative connotation. We speak of superpowers, of powerful weapons, and of the precarious balance of power in modern life. Liberation movements frequently focus on negative power structures and power bases generally attributed to the oppressing majority. Such movements hope to wrest power from oppressors in order to change the lot of the oppressed or the "powerless." "Power to the people" is a common expression of this desire for liberation, whatever the particular movement. Those who stand outside a particular movement because of race or sex or creed or ideology, however, sometimes find discussions of power either embarrassing or frightening.

Believing Lord Acton's statement is true—that power corrupts and that absolute power corrupts absolutely—we tend to eschew power and pretend it is not among our prized possessions. But how then are we to understand the Gospel? Throughout the Scriptures we discover the man Jesus as a person of extraordinary power, life-sustaining and life-generating power, in marked contrast to the death-dealing forces around him. Jesus was one from whom "power went out." Why then, as disciples of Jesus, are we uncomfortable with discussions of power and rarely willing to claim the power that is ours? Are we to believe that power goes out from Jesus but not from us? Do we pray "thine is the kingdom and the power and the glory" and absolve ourselves from the exercise of the God-given power which is ours?

So conscious are many in the contemporary Church of

the vast potential for the abuse of power within the community of believers that we have attempted to conceive models and patterns of prayer without designated leadership, perhaps attempting to eliminate coercion or manipulation of the assembly by disallowing the exercise of individual leadership. Assumptions about the uses and abuses of power in Christian life and liturgy must be examined in these times of transition when new modes of leadership are beginning to emerge. But the questions remain: is a leaderless assembly possible? Is shared leadership desirable? Would we be less reluctant to vest authority (and thus the exercise of power) in one person if we could conceive of the leadership of prayer as an exercise of power in the name of Jesus?

Surely the same power at work in Jesus can be released in those who name themselves disciples. Part of the vocation of a Christian community is to release the power of God at work in one another—not to **overpower**, which is death-dealing, but to **empower**, which is life-sustaining. Leadership of prayer is one means of empowering others, one means of freeing and facilitating the community's response to God's initiative in its midst. It is an exercise of the use of power.

Regarding leadership of prayer specifically, and the development of new models of such leadership, the question is often posed whether there should be individual leadership at all? Should one person assume leadership of the community's prayer when all of us, by gift and grace, respond to God's initiative in prayer. Should not leadership be shared in order to mirror the many gifts of the assembly as well as our desire "not to lord it over others." In those communities which have attempted to grapple seriously with such questions, a model of shared leadership has begun to emerge, a model in which first one, then another, assumes the presidency of the assembly. One person, for example, might introduce the prayer, another lead the introductory rite, another read and preach the word, and another lead the community's ritual response.

One wonders, however, whether this model touches the heart of the question which may have little to do with the number of leaders, and everything to do with *the man-*

ner in which leadership is exercised. Is it not equally possible for a number of people to abuse authority as it is for an individual? When leadership is understood as service, the number of people exercising it becomes a moot point.

Furthermore, we can learn something on this topic from those who explore ritual activity from the viewpoint of the social sciences. Is it not true, prescinding from an ecclesial framework for the moment, that from a purely sociological perspective, every group needs a leader? It is virtually axiomatic to speak of emerging leadership. In any group, whether roles have been assigned or sometimes only assumed, leadership emerges. We naturally look for someone to facilitate, to speak when a chorus of voices would be cacaphony, to orchestrate the life of the group, or simply to move us through an agenda.

Why, then, would we not admit of the same need in a gathering for prayer and turn to one among us to orchestrate the movements and order the many gifts? The fundamental question here is not whether it is more appropriate for one or several people to exercise leadership in any given service, but whether such authority is exercised as an act of loving service.

These are not simple issues, nor has the last word been spoken in the debate about authority, power and leadership. Perhaps, however, Martin Buber's reflection on the relationship of power and love may help to summarize the challenge which here confronts us:

> Our hope is too new and too old—
> I do not know what would remain to us
> Were love not transfigured power
> And power not straying love.
>
> Do not protest: "Let love alone rule!"
> Can you prove it true?
> But resolve: Every morning
> I shall concern myself anew about the boundary
> Between the love-deed-Yes and the power-deed-No
> And pressing forward honor reality.

We cannot avoid
Using power,
Cannot escape the compulsion
To afflict the world,
So let us, cautious in diction
And mighty in contradiction,
Love powerfully.[3]

The struggle to submit one's authority and power in service to the community's prayer is the work of a lifetime. Learning to love powerfully, participating in Jesus' life of obedience, and putting on the mind and heart of Christ, are ways of naming a life of continuous conversion under the tutelage of the Spirit. In the last analysis, what is important for a leader of prayer is fidelity to the journey.

THE DISCIPLINE OF CREATIVITY

Discipline does not disappear forever, but she does take vacations from time to time. By nature she is a conservative person, and yet she lives a radical life. Guided by a sense of inner necessity, she works hard and takes many risks. When Discipline was a teenager too poor to afford dance classes, she skipped lunch to pay for her lessons.

Discipline has a strong sense of order. However, when things are too neat she feels compelled to mess them up. She has a complex relationship to form. She appreciates the necessity and the dangers of structure. She understands that the same structure which supports you can also hold you back. The bones of the skeleton which support the body can become the bars of the cage which imprison the spirit. After Discipline has mastered a form, she is free to improvise.

J. Ruth Gendler, *The Book of Qualities*[4]

"After Discipline has mastered a form, she is free to improvise." "Mastery of form" and "freedom of improvisation" will be the focal points of the following pages.

Perhaps the most daunting of all aspects of lay leadership of prayer is the apparently spontaneous nature of the task. Often such leadership is summoned with little forewarning: a word of praise, a moment of blessing, a time of thanksgiving. These are recurring situations wherever two or three are gathered together in the name of the Lord. It seems so effortless when other people are called upon in such situations—but *please* don't ask me. I wouldn't know where to begin.

Then there are the longer services: catechumenal rites,

wake and graveside services, penance services, visits to the sick and communion services—not to mention Sunday services of Word and Communion in the absence of a priest. Where does one begin to prepare for the innumerable situations which will confront lay leaders of prayer in the coming years? It may appear that some of these situations require such *ad hoc* leadership that leaders of prayer have to spring into action instantaneously, creating prayer on demand. It should be consoling at the outset of this chapter to state that such is just the opposite of the art of presiding. One becomes a competent and creative presider at prayer first of all by immersing oneself in the Church's tradition and learning reverence for the ways that Christians have prayed and celebrated together for two thousand years.

A leader of prayer needs to master the Church's traditional patterns of worship and become steeped in the community's repertoire of signs and symbols and words and gestures. Fledgling presiders need to discover the ways in which basic forms of prayer have evolved over the centuries, and learn how different patterns of prayer may be created by juxtaposing various elements of the Church's tradition.

Appropriation of the Church's traditional patterns of worship requires: 1) learning the basic structure of individual "units" of prayer such as a collect, a blessing, a litany, a credal statement, intercessory prayer; 2) exploring the "languages" of postures and symbols most often used in celebration; 3) becoming sensitive to basic principles of ritual activity; and 4) having mastered the forms, finally beginning to improvise models of prayer which respect the tradition from which they have developed.

All of that is a tall order, and impossible to address through this brief work. Yet it is possible to point a direction. Consequently, in the following pages, each area of competence just outlined will be explored through at least one pastoral example. It is hoped that this will prepare the reader for further study and appropriation of traditional patterns of prayer. Such a mastery is critical if one is to become genuinely at ease and competent as a leader of prayer.

1) Learning the basic structure of individual "units" of prayer

The most ubiquitous, and thus most useful, pattern of prayer is the "collect-style" prayer. It is a pattern which appears regularly in the celebration of the Mass and the sacraments and has also come to be called a "presidential prayer." The name "collect" comes from the Latin *collecta*, which indicates its function, that is, to gather up, collect, and draw to a close the individual prayers of the assembly. This title and subsequent function suggest that a collect will be successful to the extent that individuals are actually allowed the time to pray before their prayers are collected. The words "Let us pray" which often precede a collect, are an invitation to the community. They need to be followed by the silence and the time to do just that.

The collect traditionally has four basic parts which can be coded: **You, who, do, through**.

You is the naming of God: an address drawn from the community's repertoire of titles for the divinity, a repertoire which continues to expand as we struggle to address the One whom we can never adequately name or know. The address is not chosen arbitrarily but is selected in relationship to the rest of the prayer. So, for example, if the focus of a prayer is a petition for God's forgiveness, "Merciful God" could be an appropriate "naming" for the prayer.

Who is the expansion of the address of God. The "who" code derives from the ancient Latin structure of the collect prayer which expanded the address of God through use of the subjunctive tense. The Latin *Deus, qui . . .* was translated in English as God, who. . . . Note how the expansion of God's name is accomplished in contemporary English through direct address:

God of mercy,
you welcome the stranger,
you make whole the leper,
you give salvation to those
who put their trust in you.[5]

One function of the 'You, who,'—the title and the expansion of the address—is to give hope to the community that the petition which follows will be heard because God has been faithful in the past. Occasionally, but far more rarely, the ancient pattern of prayer varies the 'who' section, not as an expansion of God's name, but in order to state the situation of the community. For example:

Patient God,
we have sinned against you
and squandered your gifts of life and grace.[6]

Finally, both expansion of the title and some statement of the community's situation might be combined as in the following text:

O God,
your ways are not our ways,
your wisdom far outruns
our human understanding.
We, your people, gather together today
to express our need for you.[7]

Do signifies the petitions which follow, petitions forcefully announced by the use of an imperative verb. Note the strength of the following:

Increase our faith:
when we are tempted to despair, sustain us;
in anxiety, console us;
in bewilderment, secure us;
and in anger, restore us to your peace.[8]

By contrast, a "may we" construction seems more like wishful thinking in God's presence than a strong plea for gracious intervention here and now in our lives. One variation of the pattern of a collect is the addition of a result clause: "do, in order that," again, a derivative of the ancient Latin construction. The use of such a result clause may strengthen the petition, as in this example:

Instruct us in the services of love,
that our hands may bring comfort to your children.
Deepen our faith in your presence,
that our eyes may recognize in each brother and sister
the face of your beloved Son.[9]

Through signals the conclusion of the prayer. The conclusion is not just tacked on, or a throw-away ending to cue the community's Amen. The content of the conclusion suggests the fundamental belief of the community that its prayer begins and ends in Jesus Christ who still intercedes on our behalf. Two forms of the conclusion are the Trinitarian and the Christological. An example of a Trinitarian conclusion would be:

Grant this through our Lord Jesus Christ, your Son,
who lives and reigns with you and the Holy Spirit,
one God, for ever and ever.

A briefer Christological conclusion might read:

Grant this through Christ our Lord.

Besides these standard forms of conclusion, it is possible to conclude the collect prayer in a more imaginative way. For example, this ending would be appropriate during Advent:

We wait for your Messiah,
keeping watch and praying in his name,
Jesus, who is Lord for ever and ever.[10]

The collect is a relatively simple pattern, which is useful in countless situations: the beginning and ending of gatherings, for concluding intercessory prayer, at table with friends. Despite this simplicity in form, however, several words of caution are in order for the composition of this and every other kind of prayer.

In 1969, the *Instruction on Translation of Liturgical Texts* noted how important it was that all members of the assembly could find and express themselves in prayer.[11] Among other things, this statement implies the necessity that the language employed in ritual prayer must be inclusive, and cannot discriminate against any member of the assembly. Such inclusivity shuns language which is racist, sexist, clericalist, antisemitic, or insensitive to the disabled.

Inclusive praying also recognizes that the naming of God has profound ramifications in shaping the consciousness of the community. While masculine imagery may have served the community in another age of the Church's life, perhaps now the best service a presider might offer is to search out new metaphors for God, thus challenging and expanding the community's relationship with our Nameless God. The Scriptures, particularly the Psalms, will provide ample examples.

Another caution was expressed years ago by Dietrich Bonhoeffer, who was aware of the awesome responsibility to express faithfully the prayer of the community:

> The free prayer in the common devotion should be the prayer of the fellowship and not that of the individual who is praying. It is [the leader's] responsibility to pray for the fellowship. So [the leader] will have to share the daily life of the fellowship; he must know the cares, the needs, the joys and thanksgivings, the petitions and hopes of others. Their work and everything they bring with them must not be unknown. . . . It will require practice and watchfulness, if [the leader] is not to confuse his own heart with the heart of the fellowship.[12]

Being attentive to the life and action of God in the community and bringing such to expression will surface again in a closing section. For now, let it suffice to suggest that any prayer which is offered is meant to touch the heart and the religious consciousness of those gathered and to elicit from them their so be it: "Amen."

A last caution for those who formulate our prayer: Improvised praise must not be a self-conscious collage of moods or feelings, but a word which expresses the *faith* and the *hope* of the gathered assembly. Such was driven home for me when Father Balthasar Fischer, during a visit to the University of Notre Dame, was fielding questions from a group of seminarians. When one questioner persisted about the development of more spontaneous eucharistic prayers, Father Fischer reminded him that it would be his privilege as presider to be as spontaneous as he wished in his preaching, but formal public prayer was different—for at the end of his preaching, no one *had* to say "Amen."

To this point we have examined the structure of one "unit" of prayer, the collect, and have noted the importance of allowing it to function *as* a collect. We have further examined some principles of composition which are equally applicable to other genre of prayer.[13] Since space does not permit a similar examination of each genre of prayer, it is hoped that this excursus may serve as a model for the study of other types of prayers. Familiarity with the structure, function, and variant forms of blessings, creeds, bidding prayers, penitential rites, litanies, and so forth, requires some knowledge of their origin and their development in the tradition. Useful, too, is some knowledge of available collections which can serve as resources. Then, "after Discipline has mastered a form, she is free to improvise," and the heart beats a little less fast when she is asked to lead common prayer.

2) Liturgical gestures and objects

How we take for granted some of the postures of our prayer! How little we reflect on the meaning of standing or sitting or folding our hands, of crossing ourselves or the triple signing at the Gospel, of processing, genuflecting and bowing our heads! Yet body language is sometimes the best and even the only language adequate to express what is in our hearts. Consider the following, a reflection on the meaning of bowing:

> "Zedekiah was one and twenty years old when he began to reign. . . . And he did that which was evil in the sight of the Lord his God, and humbled not himself before Jeremiah the prophet speaking from the mouth of the Lord . . . but he stiffened his neck and hardened his heart from turning unto the Lord God of Israel. . . . "

Unbending, unyielding,
unacknowledging of God or man.

Without a supple neck
how could I greet a neighbor in a crowd?
how could I tell my child she is doing well?
how could I express my grief and shame?
how could I assent without interrupting?
how could I show sadness in the face of suffering?
how could I show solidarity with one who speaks?
how could I offer my silent respect to a great lady?
how could I honor an eminent man?
how could I accept the verdict of my peers?
. . . simply, silently, wordlessly?

how could I surrender to the blessing
  of the One who alone can deliver me out of death?

how could I acknowledge
  that there is only one Name
  by which I can be saved—
  the name of Jesus?[14]

Enough said. What remains for the future leader of prayer is an examination of the various postures which Christians assume in prayer so as to perform them thoughtfully once again. In addition, prayer leaders need to be at ease with their own bodies and become aware that all movement in prayer is poetic rather than functional.

A variety of exercises might help. For example, the Psalms are filled with virtually every human emotion. A psalm might be read while the body attempts to express the joy or anguish, elation or anger of the psalmist. Are the hands open or clenched? the eyes closed or open? the body bowed or standing? the arms outstretched or limp? Maintain the posture. What does it call to mind? What does it surface in the heart?

A second exercise might similarly prove helpful. While music is played let the body respond to the movements of the music or the meaning of the lyrics. Yet another exercise could include imaginative reflection on a particular posture, open hands for example, and attempts to capture the experience in some poetic form. In any case, leaders of prayer will need to rehearse specific gestures before a mirror or a helpful critic, feeling their body as it assumes one or other posture of greeting, blessing or hands uplifted in prayer, known as the *orans* posture of prayer. The task is to become just as comfortable with the body language of prayer as with the oral language of prayer.

Concern for liturgical objects, another area of competence, is closely linked to the discussion of movement and gesture. Reverence for symbols begins with the recognition that the primary experience of the sacred, the primary symbol of the sacred, is the assembly. Thus an overriding concern of the leader of prayer in planning and presiding is to reverence those with whom one prays, and to make choices about every object that will be seen, touched, tasted, smelled, and heard in light of these holy ones.

Reverence for symbols includes rediscovering the many layers of meaning in the ancient symbols of the community such as food, water, oil, fire, ashes, incense, candles, and flowers. Reverence means using natural materials, being attentive to the environment, and caring for the tiniest details of arrangement. It affects the ways in which these objects are carried or displayed, and presumes that they will work their way into our deepest consciousness and our prayer:

These flowers
standing about the table
teach us to be simple
the most perfect of gifts.
It is not our toiling or our spinning
or our gathering into barns
which have place at this Eucharist,
nor even our burnt sacrifices
and sin offerings.
It is being ourselves like Jesus
which is the fitting gift—
God's will done in us.
And when done most perfectly, most freely,
we will be simple.
'Tis a gift.[15]

The same kinds of imaginative exercises used to break open the meaning of various postures might be used to expand one's consciousness and appreciation of liturgical objects and their appropriate use, that is, 1) reflection on various symbols, perhaps using Guardini's *Sacred Signs*[16]; 2) rehearsal of the actual use of oil, water, ashes, and so on; and 3) an evaluation and critique of the experience.

3) Basic Principles of Planning and Celebration

When one begins to lead services longer than a single prayer, many choices have to be made. The following pages will examine a short segment of a service, an introductory rite, in order to discuss and illustrate some of the basic principles of ritual activity and the subsequent choices which need to be made in the ritual process.

It almost goes without saying that a group gathered for prayer needs a way to begin. We need some decisive word or gesture, some movement or song which gives a signal to the assembly that together we are marking the beginning of our prayer. As Christians we have begun our prayer in various ways, for example, by tracing a sign of the cross on our bodies while reciting a Trinitarian formula, by engaging in elaborate processions accompanied by song, or simply, as on Good Friday, with the stark gesture of prostration in utter silence.

Perhaps what needs underscoring is not that we need to find a way to begin, but that the way we find should respect appropriate ritual patterns. At the moment of prayer's beginning we are not simply calling a meeting to order. Though there is something of that in an introductory rite, it is much more.

We begin our prayer by confessing God-with-us, by designating a certain time and space as sacred, by putting aside what divides us, by finding ways to acknowledge that together we are united in praise of our God, and in all that we do, by preparing ourselves to accept the blessing which springs from God's action in our midst. Thus, our first principle: the introduction, just as everything we do and say in our celebration, is liturgical action with a very different purpose than any "secular analogue."

Not only must we search for appropriate ritual behavior, but the choices we make should be to scale. This is our second principle. Scale proves to be so decisive in the choices which we must make regarding prayer forms, that it is important to pause here and clarify this concept.

To speak of scale is to suggest that many decisions will be affected by what is appropriate 1) in this particular space; 2) with this number of people assembled; 3) with whatever time constraints have been imposed on this gathering; 4) with this particular degree of solemnity or informality; 5) with the purpose of this gathering in mind; and 6) in keeping with the expectations of this community. Scale dictates both the tone and the volume of one's voice, the choice between vesture or street clothes, the size of one's gestures, the selection and number of assisting ministers, the way we arrange the furniture, and even whether there will be a rehearsal.

Perhaps another way to clarify the concept of scale is to suggest that there is no such thing as a "generic" celebration. Each time we begin to shape prayer, the needs and expectations of a very concrete community must be taken into account. Communal prayer will be "to scale" when the physical, psychological, and spiritual "demographics" of the community have been thoroughly reverenced and respected.

In applying this principle to the planning of introductory rites, we might say that in small, informal gatherings a simple moment of silence and centering might be a most appropriate way to begin prayer. Any kind of "entrance procession" in such circumstances might appear ludicrous. Contrarily, a casual "Good morning" or a "Hi and how are you?" in a large assembly will likely be met with silence. Neither of these choices is "to scale."

To make an appropriate choice we need to ask: what is the function of an introduction and what are some alternative ways of respecting this function? The *Directory for Masses with Children*, citing the *General Instruction of the Roman Missal*, describes the function of an introductory rite and then offers several principles to guide planning:

The introductory rite of Mass has as its purpose "that the faithful coming together take on the form of a community and prepare themselves to listen to God's word and celebrate the eucharist properly." (GIRM 24) Therefore every effort should be made to create this disposition in the children and not to jeopardize it by any excess of rites in this part of Mass.

It is sometimes proper to omit one or other element of an introductory rite or perhaps to expand one of the elements. There should always be at least some introductory element, which is completed by the opening prayer. In choosing individual elements, care should be taken that each one be used from time to time and that none be entirely neglected.[17]

Clearly that statement applies, with appropriate adaptation, to any form of ritual prayer. It notes that the function of an introductory rite is to assist a group of people in experiencing themselves as a community and in preparing themselves to listen and respond to God in common prayer, a function best served by simplicity rather than excess. This caution is well taken. It is very tempting to overload an introductory moment, trying to make it bear the weight of the entire service. We experience ourselves as a community, however, not by the number of things we do together but by the quality and the tone of those few elements which enable our gathering.

How is the experience of community fostered? Some explicit interaction among the members is helpful such as greeting one another, communal singing, or ritual dialogue. In addition, the very attitude of the leader will foster or hinder participation to the degree that the leader makes the service the prayer of everyone, therein recognizing the need for mutual attentiveness and respect among the worshippers.

A second function of the introduction is to enable the community to listen and respond to God's presence. It may be helpful to recall the many modes of Christ's presence articulated by the *Constitution on the Sacred Liturgy*, that is: in the gathered assembly, in the minister, in the proclaimed Word, in the Bread of Life and the Cup of Salvation.[18] The types of listening to which the community is called are thus manifold as are the possibilities for our response, for example, through silence, song, reading, prayer, gesture, and ritual action.

Given these various possibilities, the *Directory* suggests several principles for selection: 1) the opening prayer is of the essence of this moment, to be accompanied by at least one other element; 2) a community should explore the many options over a period of time, not ignoring any of the traditional ways for beginning prayer; 3) by implication, a particular feast, season, or occasion may help to shape the beginning of common prayer. Music, for example, would always be selected with a specific feast, season or ritual moment in mind. Other elements might be reserved to a particular season, such as the penitential rites to the season of Lent.

In all cases, and here we can generalize beyond the introductory rites, the elements chosen for a rite are for the sake of the gathered community, to help experience themselves as "pray-ers" before the Holy One, attentive to God's presence and open to response. Simplicity and variety are further key principles for ritual planning which can support the worship of the community and not impede the movement of the Spirit. That may sound like a great burden on those who plan. Yet it may be consoling, in this regard, to remember the words of Preface IV for weekdays:

You have no need of our praise,
yet our desire to thank you is itself your gift.[19]

All is gift, even the desire to turn to God in prayer. Planning appropriate ritual response is, above all, an act of attentiveness to the word momentarily addressed to these people, and a freeing of the response with which God has *already* graced the community.

What if all that has been asked is a simple prayer? How would that be introduced? The same principles apply as above, but on a smaller scale. So, for example, a group can experience themselves as a community if they engage in a brief ritual dialogue such as, "The Lord be with you. And also with you. Let us pray," followed by a period of silence. The leader then "collects" the silent prayer of the community, bringing to expression the listening and response of each heart, enabling a verbal affirmation: "Amen." The Preface dialogue is also useful for a slightly more elaborate introduction to a collect prayer.

Finally, effective ritual activity requires balance, quality, variety, tone, and pace. How are these learned? Perhaps the best means of learning why some prayer is "successful"—an unhappy word, but the meaning is clear—and why some prayer leaves us empty is to become aware of the evaluation that goes on all of the time but is rarely brought to conscious expression. We leave a celebration of whatever kind and in the car or over the dinner table remarks are made about this or that element, what was liked and what was not liked. But the question should always be posed—why? Why did you find that prayer so moving? Why did the music seem to create just the right atmosphere? Why did you feel you were rushed through the service, even though it was no shorter than others of its type? Why did the space seem to stifle you or release your spirit? What was there about the words of blessing which touched you?

A second and absolutely indispensable means of discovering the principles of planning and celebration is to read and reread several recent documents on the liturgy. As was demonstrated above, the *Directory for Masses with Children* contains principles neither exclusively for children nor only applicable at Mass. Similarly, documents on *Environment and Art, Music in Catholic Worship, The Introduction to the Lectionary*, and *The General Norms for the Liturgical Year*, are all filled with principles which lay leaders of prayer will find instructive and useful for the development of a ritual sense.

4) Improvisation

"After Discipline has mastered a form she is free to improvise." Why? Because ritual prayer is not created out of whole cloth. It will only be ritual prayer if it draws on the tradition, if it contains repetitive patterns identifiable to the participants. Even in the early Church, when romantic revisionists think Christian prayer was spontaneous and from the heart, nevertheless the community drew on patterns of proclamation and response, prayer dialogues, spatial arrangements, and musical repertoire already familiar as part of our Jewish heritage.

For a lay leader of prayer, improvisation is an ability to reverence the tradition and to draw on familiar structures and styles of celebration, perhaps combining them in new ways for new ritual occasions. In most situations, the lay leader is not constrained by canons and rubrics governing appropriate sacramental patterns of prayer. There is no *Rituale* and no *ordo*. The lay leader thus has great freedom in planning and celebration, but a freedom tempered by responsibility to the community she or he serves.

One of the challenges facing a lay presider is the need to collect and assimilate all of the resources already available for the various forms of prayer which require this ministry. Few resources are directed specifically to the lay presider, and yet numerous resources are available to assist us if we can overcome a certain reluctance to use and adapt the existing liturgical books. *The Rites of the Catholic Church*, for example, should be on the shelf of each presider, lay or ordained. For the lay presider, this collection contains all of the rites of the catechumenate, several model reconciliation services, wonderful resources for the pastoral care of the sick, and prayers for the dying and the dead.[20] Not only does each of these rites include appropriate prayers but to each is appended a selection of Scripture references.

Similarly, *The Sacramentary* is a rich resource for prayers: collects, penitential rites, simple and solemn blessings, intercessory prayers, greetings, and prayers for a variety of needs and occasions. Some of the editions of *The Sacramentary* also contain a number of the liturgical documents cited above for study. In addition, a variety of resources are appended to this essay, and many are extremely helpful for the development of creative patterns of worship. None of them, however, is as helpful as the ritual books of the community which belong to all of us, clergy and laity alike.

A final word about planning. Planning is less linear than it is circular. By that I mean that the first question should never be "what shall we sing to start?" but "what are we celebrating?" What is the occasion in the life of the community for which a service of prayer is desired? An example may help to flesh this out.

Our faculty goes away overnight at the beginning of each academic year for what are called faculty study days. These days have a variety of goals, one of which is to affirm and deepen our sense of work as ministry. How shall we celebrate that? The days would be filled with words. Why not have at the heart of our prayer a ritual gesture in silence, that is, the anointing of one another. Now begins the planning in spiral. If the heart of a service is a ritual gesture in silence, perhaps a Scripture passage might introduce the gesture. We chose "The Spirit of the Lord is upon me. . . . " from Isaiah 61. These two elements now became the center of the prayer. Then other questions could be raised: how shall we arrange the room? who would preside? could we bless the oil together? should music be used to set the tone? would a simple mantra, perhaps the *Veni, Sancte Spiritus* of Taizé, express our prayer for one another and for the year ahead? How would we bring this moment of prayer to a conclusion?

Such is spiral planning: What are we celebrating? How do we want to ritualize that? What is the core or the heart of our prayer? What will be the role of silence, reading, response? How will mutuality and participation be fostered? What is the scale? How shall we begin? How shall we conclude?

Good "improvisation" is not usually done on the spur of the moment. It is a competency born of knowledge, reverence, and ease. It takes the best of our liturgical heritage and places it in faithful dialogue with the invitation of God to *this* community, at *this* moment of its history, to listen and to respond.

THE LEADER AS ICON[21]

"Put your gifts at the service of one another, each in the measure received."

1 Pet. 4:10

It is perilous to discuss the "spirituality of a leader of prayer" for a number of reasons. A first peril is obvious. In our day "spirituality" is a word as frequently used and abused as are "discernment," "ministry," "dialogue," "process," "community," and "sharing." "Spirituality" belongs to the linguistic category of "theological babblegab," empty of meaning because of thoughtless usage. For our purposes, spirituality will simply mean one's experience of God in faith and the way one responds concretely to God within a community of believers. It is hoped that through concrete examples this simple definition will become clear.

A second peril in discussing spirituality in light of one's relationship with God is that the latter is not a univocal category. Having a relationship with God has taken on remarkable diversity because of the variety of peoples, temperaments, historical periods, schools, movements, and above all, because of the work of the Spirit in the heart of individuals and communities alike. My spirituality and yours, though possibly born in the same geographical, historical and theological environment, will most likely be articulated differently. While we both have an experience of God to whom we respond in faith, the God we experience is like a precious gem held up to the light. I see one facet, you another; I am drawn to one aspect of the unfathomable mystery who is God, you to another. Thus, my response and yours will be nuanced differently, attesting to the remarkable richness and pluriformity of spiritualities.

What follows is therefore simply *one* way to ground prayer leadership, one approach to spirituality. It will serve its purpose if it encourages readers consciously to explore their own experiences of God which may give flesh to their way of serving God's community by enabling its sacrifice of praise.

The starting point for a spirituality of a prayer leader, as implied earlier, is Christ who stands before the throne of grace, the Christ who is the perfect revelation of God, the Christ who is First Born of all creation. Christ serves as *the* leader of prayer because he is a kind of two-way icon as so exquisitely portrayed in Second Corinthians: "For all the promises of God find their Yes in him. That is why we utter the Amen through him, to the glory of God." (2 Cor 1:20)

Christ is the perfect leader of prayer, the perfect mediator before God, because he is so perfectly attuned to God and to the human community, so perfectly the Word of God and the Amen we would declare. It is he in whom the fullness of God was pleased to dwell and yet the One who did not cling to equality with God but emptied himself and became one of us. (Phil 2:6–7) Christ is not a high priest unable to sympathize with our weakness but one who is himself beset by weakness. (Heb 5:2)

This too brief Christological foundation for leadership of prayer suggests two things. First, the whole life and ministry of Jesus must serve as a model for the leader of prayer. Second, the ultimate function of a leader of prayer is to be that same two-way icon: serving both to reveal the face of God within the community, and to speak the Amen to God in the name of the community. Let us examine each of these facets of leadership in turn.

1) Jesus' life and ministry

Every aspect of the earthly life of Jesus—his preaching, healing, prayer, and submission to the will of the one whom he called Abba culminating in passion, death and final glorification—was directed to the realization of the reign of God. Jesus revealed God and realized God's saving will in *all* that he was, said and did. His life and his ministry of proclamation and service provide the paradigm for any of us who would attach ourselves to Jesus and claim to be his disciples. How much more do they serve as a model for one who would minister in Jesus' name for the building up of the Body of Christ, when the people of God assemble in faith. The leader of prayer has first to believe and to act upon the Gospel before he or she can begin to lead others in prayer.

One might be tempted at this point to throw in the towel! Lord, who can be saved! Lord, who could possibly lead your people? We might take great comfort in the promise expressed in the Fourth Eucharistic Prayer which gives a wonderful summary of Jesus' way of life:

> To the poor he proclaimed the good news of salvation,
> to prisoners, freedom,
> and to those in sorrow, joy.
> In fulfillment of your will
> he gave himself up to death;
> but by rising from the dead,
> he destroyed death and restored life.

And then, even as it acknowledges our selfishness and our need, it expresses words of hope and promise:

> And that we might live no longer for ourselves but for him,
> he sent the Holy Spirit from you, Father,
> as his first gift to those who believe,
> to complete his work on earth
> and bring us the fullness of grace.[22]

We are promised the Spirit; we are promised the fullness of grace. Trusting in the fidelity of God and acting in the power of the Spirit our hearts will be tutored in submission to God and in compassion for God's people. Thus we will begin to "complete Christ's work on earth," a vocation which must be sustained and renewed regularly in assemblies for prayer.

2) The Leader of Prayer as icon

Earlier we described Jesus' mediatorial role as, in part, iconic: Jesus is Word and revelation of God. Jesus is our perfect Amen, the one who helps us to draw near to God with faith and confidence, the one whose Spirit knows our weakness and who prays within us. Jesus is God's word to us and our word to God. How does the leader of prayer participate in this iconic vocation?

The General Instruction on the Roman Missal speaks of this role explicitly. "By his [her] actions and by his [her] proclamations of the word he [the leader of prayer] should impress upon the faithful the living presence of Christ."[23] One who would lead the assembly's prayer must first strive to be a person alive to the presence of God, attentive to the myriad ways in which the Holy One is manifested in human life. Consistent patterns of personal prayer will foster a contemplative, reverential awareness of the wonder of God gradually working a grace-filled transformation in oneself. Moreover, the contemplative leader of prayer will be led beyond self to an awareness of the Spirit of God active in the community that believes, hopes, dreams, struggles, and suffers together.

Alive to the reality of prayer, reverent before the Holy One, alert to the mystery of the Presence whenever and wherever it is manifested, leaders of prayer will be able to discern within themselves and within human events the traces and signs of God in the midst of the community. The leader of prayer will be icon of God to the community to the extent that he or she is personally attuned to that Presence.

Let there be no misunderstanding. The search for God is no remote or isolated venture. If leaders of prayer are not at home wandering around their own hearts, if they are not attuned to joy in the presence of friends, if they have not been startled by the wonder of life or surprised by the fragility of all creation, then their public prayer will likewise be impoverished. If they have not grieved at the death of a friend or been humbled by another's love; if they have not known compassion for the weak, or been stirred by a smile of innocence; if they have not been moved or amazed by all of these, then will their prayer likewise be hollow. If they have not discovered their own emptiness without God; if they have not admitted the reality of their own sinfulness; if they have not grieved the alienation which sin effects; if they have not pondered humankind's capacity for destruction and betrayal; if they do not stand in horror of all of these, then their prayer in the assembly will be empty and incapable of giving voice to the inner prayer of those gathered. Leaders of prayer will be icons of the community's prayer before God only to the extent that they are in touch with the human need and longing for God that lie deep in their own and every human heart.

Our prayer comes from the stuff of our daily lives. It is there that we find traces of our often hidden God speaking eloquently between the lines of our existence. God is discovered above all in that place most familiar to us—a place which is the most sacred and dangerous for a leader of prayer—the place of our own humanity.

QUALITIES AND SKILLS

To this point we have suggested that leadership of prayer consists in announcing the presence of God and in facilitating the community's response. It is clear that the authentic leader of prayer must be animated—in life as in liturgy—by a continuous search for the presence of the Holy One in order that she or he may enable our discovery of that presence and our surrender in faith. Now we can become more concrete in describing particular qualities and skills demanded of the leader which flow from this mandate.

There are many ways of announcing the presence of God. Prayer leaders are called to announce God's presence by their actions and their words. They exercise leadership by presiding over the assembly, voicing its prayer, proclaiming the message of salvation, enabling the community's response to God-with-us, and sending the community to live what it has proclaimed. Such exercise of leadership is true whether the celebration is a Eucharist, a service of Word and Communion, a Penance service, Sunday Vespers, or any of the communal prayer services in our repertoire.

Presidency of the assembly begins long before the scheduled hour of celebration. It is the responsibility of the leader of prayer to take a leading role in planning the celebration with the other ministers and all who have a special responsibility for the community's prayer. As one who will normally participate in the planning meeting, the leader of prayer must be equipped for this ministry by prayerful reflection on the Word of God, a solid mastery of the revised rites, and an intimate knowledge of the celebrating community. The prayer of the Church is always the prayer of some actual community assembled here and now. The presider must be aware of that community and the ways in which God is touching its members in their daily lives.

Particular abilities required for the planning process include a certain degree of organizational skill, effectiveness in group process, flexibility and creativity. Furthermore, presiders are called upon to inspire the planning process by the transparency of their own faith, their understanding of the Church's prayer traditions, and their personal concern for the community being served.

Throughout the celebration, leaders exercise the presidency of the assembly by accommodating their greetings and other introductions to the particular congregation, by assuming their own role and orchestrating the other ministries, by directing the community's attention to other ministers through their own bearing and attentiveness, by inviting its participation and dwelling in its stillness. Leaders of prayer unite the community, direct its celebration, and enable the diverse ministries carried on in its daily life to come to full expression in the celebration.

A leader of prayer also "announces" the presence of God in the assembly through the proclamation of prayer in the community's name. Within the liturgical event there are various modes of communication, different kinds of speech and silence. Leaders of prayer may address God in personal, private prayer or in the name of the assembly. They may address the community informally, for example, introductions, or formally, for example, invitations to prayer. They may become part of the assembly in prayers that belong to the entire congregation, blending their voice with the community's chorus of praise and prayer, for example, the Our Father. Presiders are also called upon to lead the community in silence and prayerful response, as well as in acts of mutual awareness and reconciliation.

Leaders must therefore be skilled in enabling these various kinds of communication to occur unambiguously within the assembly. This requires familiarity with the inner structure of various rites and the interrelationship of their many parts as well as a keen awareness of the mode of communication appropriate to the moment. At those moments when leaders are allowed spontaneity, they should use such freedom with care, not substituting sermonettes when brief communication is required, not allowing their own moods to transpose a moment of formal prayer into quasi-private communication, not using stilted language when a personal word is appropriate or breezy informality when a public word is required.

Prayer in the name of the community is a grace-filled moment, not a memorized formula or a text upon a printed page. The many modes of human communication in prayer are invitations for loving surrender to the One who makes this coming together so holy.

Because of the nature of communal prayer itself, the presider must be present to the assembly, inviting and encouraging their participation. As *the* community person, the leader of prayer should neither apologize for this ministry nor dominate the assembly. Leadership is an exercise of service, not of power. Presiders are called to orchestrate a diversity of community ministries and they are neither expected nor able to carry alone the responsibility for the community's affairs during or outside of the celebration.

Prayer leaders create an atmosphere of reverence for the sacramentality of word, gesture and object. They attempt to develop their own ritual sense and allow symbols to speak out of their own richness. They respect the many modes of communication and become neither chummy nor individualistic. Leaders of prayer accept themselves and are at ease within the community. They are spontaneous in their service rather than rigid, self-conscious or remote. Their ecclesiology recognizes that all share in the priesthood of Christ and that all are concelebrants of the community's prayer. Their image of community depicts a group of people who listen to one another, befriend each other, and share life together.

As servants to believing communities, leaders of prayer place the transparency of their own faith at the service of others, while they encourage a genuine dialogue of faith which prepares and prolongs worship in spirit and in truth. They gladly accept responsibility for the tradition of the Church's prayer and adapt the rites to the need and expectations of their local assemblies.

Leaders of prayer care for the continuity between the worship of God in communal celebration and the service of God's kingdom in the world. They promote regular reflection on what it means to be a disciple of the Lord Jesus in word, prayer, and service. Thus do they show that liturgy is not a stepping outside of one's daily life, but rather is a true expression of one's life in the Lord.

SUMMARY

It should be abundantly clear as we conclude these reflections that leadership of prayer is not a matter of whim. It is not for the personal aggrandizement of the one who would seize it, nor is it an optional structure, to be discharged indiscriminately by anyone in the assembly. Leaders of prayer are chosen by the community because of their obvious gift and grace. They are disciples of Jesus, aware that they, like Jesus, are beset by weakness. Yet in that very fragility they are willing to place their gifts at the service of the community in the same measure in which they have been received. Because of the transparency of the leader's faith it is the Amen of Christ to which we join our voice for the glory of God when we gather for prayer.

Fundamentally it is *always* and *ultimately* Christ who leads our assemblies and invites us to praise and thanksgiving, who speaks the word and makes possible our prayer. It must be the ceaseless effort of every leader of prayer to ponder what God-with-us means. Thus will we be faithful heralds of Christ's presence, power and love in our assemblies.

GUIDELINES FOR THE COMPOSITION OF ORIGINAL PRAYERS[24]

Function and Structure

1. The author should keep in mind the function of the prayer, its place and purpose in the rite.

2. The prayers are intended for **proclamation** in the liturgical assembly.

3. While the traditional elements of a particular genre of prayer (e.g., the classic order of a collect contains address, amplification of address, petition, result clause, conclusion) should be contained in the newly composed prayers, they need not in every instance follow exactly the structure of the prayers now in the *Sacramentary* or other ritual books.

4. The thoughts expressed in the prayers should have a logical coherence and unity and the prayers should have a coherent structure.

5. The nature of the rite as well as the moment in the rite and its ritual context will influence the tone of the prayer.

Content and Style

6. The prayers must be doctrinally sound.

7. Inspiration for the prayers will be found in the Scriptures, the seasons and the theology underlying the various rites. For example, references to baptism would be expected in some presidential prayers in Lent and the Easter season.

8. The prayers should have enough substance to draw the congregation into prayer and to afford inspiration for meditation.

9. The themes of the prayers should be fairly universal so that they can be used in a variety of places and circumstances. These compositions are usually prepared for a varied community and should avoid themes that might be suitable for a particular group or region but would be meaningless or confusing in other circumstances.

10. As far as possible the author should avoid moving from the concrete to the abstract in prayer composition. A concrete prayer is one that is rooted in human experience and speaks of basic human concerns. Thus rooted in human experience, a prayer can be concrete and universal at the same time.

11. The prayers should be clear, forceful, interesting, consistent and imaginative.

12. There should be a consistency of images, and care must be exercised not to use too many images in a single prayer, lest the hearers become confused.

13. An effort should be made to open the prayers to a wide-ranging vocabulary. Color and poetic imagery, where possible, should be evident in compositions. At the same time jargon or esoteric words should be avoided.

14. The prayers should use inclusive language and avoid the use of language which may discriminate on sexist, racist, clericalist or anti-Semitic grounds.

15. Attention to rhythm and cadence must be a primary consideration in the composition of new prayers.

16. Prayers should be written in sense lines with a view to their being proclaimed well, heard, and easily understood.

17. Authors should avoid stock-in-trade collect phrases (e.g., vouchsafe, beseech, etc.).

18. Original prayers should in general be fuller and give more time for assimilation of their content than the traditional, brief collect.

19. Christian liturgical prayer is traditionally directed to the First Person of the Trinity, through the mediation of the Son, in the power of the Spirit.

20. Care must be taken to respect the Trinitarian economy. Traditional titles ordinarily ascribed to one Person are not used for another Person (e.g., the Spirit is the Comforter).

21. Within the prayers references to the different Persons of the Trinity must be expressed clearly, especially when pronouns (e.g., you, he) are being used.

22. Authors are encouraged to incorporate a wide range of metaphors, especially those drawn from the Scriptures, in the forms of address of the prayers. The choice of address should be made bearing in mind the content of the balance of the prayer.

23. While presidential prayers are traditionally addressed to the First Person of the Trinity, there are other genres (e.g. litanies) which may be addressed to the Son or the Spirit.

24. Attention must be given to the conclusions of the prayers in order that they express the mediation of Christ. The conclusion, whether standard or more inventive, should fit with what has gone before in the body of the prayers. It may be interwoven within the prayer. If there is a doxology in the body of the prayer, it seems best to omit a full doxology in the conclusion.

NOTES

[1]Robert Hovda, *Strong, Loving and Wise: Presiding in Liturgy*, 5th ed. (Washington: The Liturgical Conference, 1983), viii.

[2] Edward Schillebeeckx and Johannes Metz, eds., *Right of the Community to a Priest*, Concilium 133 (New York: The Seabury Press, 1980).

[3]Martin Buber, *A Believing Humanism*, trans. Maurice Friedman (New York: Simon and Schuster, 1967), p. 45.

[4]J. Ruth Gendler, *The Book of Qualities* (Berkeley: Turquoise Mountain Publications, 1984), p. 11.

[5]International Commission on English in the Liturgy, *Presidential Prayers for Experimental Use at Mass* (Washington: ICEL, 1983), p. 18.

[6]Ibid., p. 10. (The address of this prayer has been changed.)

[7]Ibid., p. 16.

[8]Ibid.

[9]Ibid., p. 22.

[10]Ibid., p. 38.

[11]*Instruction on the Translation of Liturgical Texts* in *Documents on the Liturgy 1963–1979: Conciliar, Papal, and Curial Texts* = [DOL #123], (Collegeville: The Liturgical Press, 1982) #20.

[12]Dietrich Bonhoeffer, *Life Together* (London: SCM Press, 1949), pp. 46–7.

[13]Additional guidelines for the composition of original prayer texts may be found in the Appendix.

[14]Mark Searle, "Bowing," *Assembly* 6:3 (1979) 79.

[15]Barbara Schmich, "Flowers," *Assembly* 8:1 (1981) 142.

[16]Romano Guardini, *Sacred Signs* (St. Louis: Pio Decimo Press, 1956).

[17]*Directory for Masses with Children*, #40 [DOL #276].

[18]*Constitution on the Sacred Liturgy*, #7 [DOL #1].

[19]"Preface for Weekdays IV," *The Sacramentary* Approved for Use in the Dioceses of the United States of America by the National Conference of Catholic Bishops and Confirmed by the Apostolic See (Collegeville: The Liturgical Press, 1974), p. 456.

[20]A revised translation of *The Order of Christian Funerals* has been submitted by the American Conference of Bishops to the Apostolic See for confirmation. Once confirmed, it will be readily available.

[21]What follows has been adapted from material which appeared previously under the title "Announcing the Presence" in *Modern Liturgy*, 13:1 (1986) 6–8.

[22]"Eucharistic Prayer IV," *The Sacramentary*, p. 519.

[23]See Congregation for Divine Worship, *The General Instruction of the Roman Missal*, #60 [DOL #208]. This paragraph refers to the many modes of announcing the presence of God within the eucharistic celebration. The principles espoused by this General Instruction are equally applicable wherever the community assembles for prayer.

[24]These Guidelines have been slightly adapted from a working paper of the International Commission on English in the Liturgy. Used with permission.

RESOURCES
LEADERSHIP OF PRAYER

Primary Resources

(Leaders of prayer should become familiar with the following resources, most if not all of which are available in each parish sacristy.)

The Rites of the Catholic Church. 2 Volumes. New York: Pueblo, 1983.

   I   Christian Initiation
      Rite of Penance
      Holy Communion and Worship of the Eucharist Outside Mass
      Rite of the Blessing of Oils. Rite of Consecrating the Chrism
      Rite of Marriage
      Pastoral Care of the Sick: Rites of Anointing and Viaticum
      Rite of Funerals

  II   Institution of Readers and Acolytes
      Ordination of Deacons, Priests, and Bishops
      Blessing of Persons
      Dedication of a Church and an Altar
      Appendices

The Order of Christian Funerals

The Sacramentary

The Lectionary

The Liturgy Documents, ed. G. Huck, 2nd ed. Chicago: Liturgy Training Publications, 1985.

The Constitution on the Sacred Liturgy
The General Instruction on the Roman Missal with the U.S.
  Appendix
General Norms for the Liturgical Year
Directory for Masses with Children
Music in the Catholic Worship
Environment and Art in Catholic Worship
Lectionary for Mass: Introduction
Liturgical Music Today

The American Book of Blessings

Secondary Resources
(And an Occasional Thoughtful Article)

(The following collection of books and articles might appear overwhelming. Few of us might be able to afford or have the time to read and master everything listed here. A leader of prayer might look over these selections and choose at least one resource from each of the categories listed below.)

Collections of Prayers and Blessings

Appleton, G. *The Oxford Book of Prayer*. Oxford: Oxford University Press, 1985.

Canadian Conference of Catholic Bishops. *A Book of Blessings*. Ottawa: CCCB, 1981.

Coughlan, P. et al. *A Christian's Prayer Book: Psalms, Poems and Prayers for the Church's Year*. Chicago: Franciscan Herald Press, 1972.

Cunningham, A. *Prayer: Personal and Liturgical*. Message of the Fathers of the Church, 16. Wilmington: Michael Glazier, 1985.

Deiss, L. *Come Lord Jesus: Biblical Prayers with Psalms and Scripture Readings*. Chicago: World Library Publications, 1976/1981.

Geissler, E., ed. *The Bible Prayer Book: All the Prayers, Songs, Hymns, Canticles, Psalms and Blessings in the Bible*. Notre Dame: Ave Maria Press, 1981.

Gittins, A. *Heart of Prayer: African, Jewish and Christian*. London: Collins, 1985.

Gjerding, I. and Kinnamon, K. *No Longer Strangers: A Resource for Women and Worship*. Geneva: WCC Publications, 1984.

Hickman, H., et al. *Handbook of the Christian Year*. Nashville: Abingdon Press, 1986.

Hilsdale, P. *Prayers From St. Paul.* New York: Sheed and Ward, 1964.

Mazziotta, R. *We Pray to the Lord: General Intercessions.* Notre Dame: Ave Maria Press, 1984.

Mbiti, J. *The Prayers of African Religions.* London: S.P.C.K., 1975.

National Sisters Vocation Conference. *Woman's Song: Prayer Services, Music and Poetry.* Chicago: N.S.V.C., 1986.

Schaffran, J. and Kozak, P. *More Than Words: Prayer and Ritual for Inclusive Communities.* 1986. (c/o Kozak, 1918 West 73rd St., Cleveland, OH 44102.)

Sergio, L. *Prayers of Women.* New York: Harper and Row, 1965.

Simons, T. *Blessings for God's People: A Book of Blessings for All Occasions.* Notre Dame: Ave Maria, 1983.

Walton, J. "Ecclesiastical and Feminist Blessing: Women as Objects and Subjects of the Power of Blessing." *Blessing and Power.* David Power and Mary Collins, eds. Concilium 178. Edinburgh: T. and T. Clark, 1985.

Winter, M. T. *Woman Prayer Woman Song: Resources for Ritual.* Oak Park, IL: Meyer Stone Books, 1987.

Family Prayer

Canadian Conference of Catholic Bishops. *Family Book of Prayer.* Ottawa: Concacan, Inc., 1983.

Curran, D. *Family Prayer.* Mystic, CT: Twenty-Third Publications, 1978.

Hays, E. *Prayers for the Domestic Church: A Handbook for Worship in the Home.* Easton, Kansas: Forest of Peace Books, Inc., 1979.

Huck, G. *A Book of Family Prayer.* San Francisco: Seabury Press, 1979.

Moser, L. *Home Celebrations.* Paramus, N.J.: Newman, 1970.

National Bulletin on Liturgy, 68 (1979). [Issue on family prayer.]

Travnikar, R. *The Blessing Cup: 24 Simple Rites for Family Prayer-Celebrations.* Cincinnati: St. Anthony Messenger Press, 1979.

Hours (and Variants)

Brothers of Taizé. *Common Prayer for Every Day.* Taizé: Les Presses de Taizé, 1981.

Christian Prayer: The Liturgy of the Hours. New York: Catholic Book Publishing, 1976/1983.

Consultation on Common Texts. *Ecumenical Services of Prayer.* New York: Paulist, 1983.

Ecumenical Services of Prayer. Prepared by the Consultation on Common Texts (CCT). New York: Paulist, 1983.

Jasper, R., ed. *The Daily Office Revised With Other Prayers and Services.* London: S.P.C.K., 1978.

Liturgy of the Hours. 4 vols. New York: Catholic Book Publishing, 1975. [In addition to the contents of *Christian Prayer,* this set includes the complete Office of Readings, as well as prayers, poetry, and intercessions that might be included in other forms of prayer.]

Melloh, J. and Storey, W. *Praise God in Song: Ecumenical Daily Prayer.* Chicago: G.I.A. Publications, 1979.

Storey, W. *Morning Praise and Evensong.* Notre Dame: Fides Publications, 1973.

Language

Hurd, R. "Complementarity: A Proposal for Liturgical Language." *Worship* 61 (1987) 386–404.

Leach, M. and Schreck, N. *Psalms Anew: A Non-Sexist Edition.* Dubuque: The Sisters of St. Francis, 1984.

Lectionary for the Christian People. eds. Gordon Lathrop and Gail Ramshaw. 3 vols. New York: Pueblo, 1986/1987/1988.

Lutheran Church in America. *Guidelines for Inclusive Language.* New York: Office of Communication, Lutheran Church in America, n.d.

Russell, L., ed. *The Liberating Word: A Guide to Non-Sexist Interpretation of the Bible.* Philadelphia: Westminster Press, 1976.

Withers, B. *Language About God in Liturgy and Scripture: A Study Guide.* Philadelphia: Geneva Press, 1980.

Lay Preaching and Presiding

Brulin, M. "Sunday Assemblies without a Priest in France: Present Facts and Future Questions." *Right of a Community to a Priest.* eds. E. Schillebeeckx and J. Metz. Concilium 133, New York: Seabury, 1980, pp. 29–36.

Burke, W. "With Excellent Voice: The Art of Reading, Speaking, Composing." *Modern Liturgy* 13 (1986) 12–13.

Carroll, M. and Cannon, K. "Enfleshing the Word: The Case for Lay Preachers." *Liturgy* 24 (1979) 31–34.

Cieslak, W. "At Home in the Sanctuary: Prayer Leadership with Style and Grace." *Modern Liturgy* 13 (1986) 9–11.

Foley, N., ed. *Preaching and the Non-Ordained.* Collegeville, MN: The Liturgical Press, 1984.

Ritual for Lay Presiders: God's Word, Thanksgiving, Communion. 2nd rev. ed. Regina: Western Liturgical Conference, 1985.

Goergen, D. "Preaching and the Non-Ordained." *Spirituality Today* 35 (1983) 59–71.

Hardin, G. *The Leadership of Worship.* Nashville: Abingdon Press, 1980.

Henderson, F. "When Lay People Preside at Sunday Worship." *Worship* 58 (1984) 108–117.

_____ . "The Minister of Liturgical Preaching." *Worship* 56 (1982) 214–230.

Hovda, R. *Strong, Loving and Wise: Presiding in Liturgy.* 5th ed. Collegeville, MN: The Liturgical Press, 1980.

Hughes, K. "Announcing the Presence." *Modern Liturgy* 13 (1986) 6–8.

National Bulletin on Liturgy, 79 (1981). [Issue on lay presiding.]

Northup, L. A. "The Woman as Presider: Images Drawn from Life." *Worship* 58 (1984) 526–530.

Park, P. "Women and Liturgy." *Women Ministers: How Women are Redefining Traditional Roles.* ed. Judith Weidman. New York: Harper and Row, 1981/1985. pp. 7–88.

Skudlarek, W. "Lay Preaching and the Liturgy." *Worship* 58 (1984) 500–506.

Van Beeck, F. J. "Praise and Thanksgiving in Noneucharistic Communion Services." *Worship* 60 (1986) 423–434.

Willimon, W. H. *Preaching and Leading Worship.* Philadelphia: The Westminster Press, 1984.

Meal Prayers

A Book of Graces. St. Paul: Daybreak Publications, 1973.

Auman, R. F. *A Handbook of Table Prayer.* Iowa Falls: CSS Publishing Company, 1972.

Bouyer, M. D. *Table Prayer.* New York: Herder and Herder, 1967.

Huck, G. *Tableprayerbook.* Chicago: Liturgy Training Publications, 1980.

McElroy, P. S. *Prayers and Graces of Thanksgiving.* White Plains, NY: Peter Pauper Press, 1966.

Tengborn, M. *Table Prayers.* Minneapolis: Augsburg Publishing, 1977.

Teresa, M. *Prayers at Mealtime.* New York: Paulist, 1972.

Reconciliation

Freburger, W. J. and Haas, J. E. *The Forgiving Christ: A Book of Penitential Celebrations.* Notre Dame: Ave Maria Press, 1977.

Jurgens, W. A. *Four Forms of a Penance Service.* Collegeville: The Liturgical Press, 1976.

Koplik, W. and Brady, J. *Celebrating Forgiveness.* Mystic, CT: Twenty-Third Publications, 1981.

Scripture Services

Chao, A., and Brunner, P. *Glory to the Lord.* Collegeville: The Liturgical Press, 1966. [20 Bible Vigils]

Gallagher, M. et al. *Praying with Scripture.* New York: Paulist, 1983.

Gallen, J. *Scripture Services.* Collegeville: The Liturgical Press, 1963. [18 Bible Themes edited for group use]

Habig, M. A. *Stand Firm in the Lord.* Chicago: Franciscan Herald Press, 1973. [33 Scripture Celebrations]

Sickness and Death

Champlin, J. *Through Death to Life: Preparing to Celebrate the Mass of Christian Burial.* Notre Dame: Ave Maria Press, 1979.

Fear Not, for I am With You. Staten Island: Alba House, 1973.

Kofler, M. and O'Connor, K. *Handbook for Ministers of Care.* Chicago: Liturgy Training Publications, 1987.

Shannon, T. and Faso, C. *Let Them Go Free: Family Prayer Service to Assist in the Withdrawal of Life Support Systems.* Kansas City, MO: Sheed and Ward, 1987.

Ziegler, John. "Who Can Anoint the Sick?" *Worship* 61 (1987) 25–44.

Varia

Assembly. The Journal of the Notre Dame Center for Pastoral Liturgy. See the issues on "Liturgical Objects," 8:1 (1981); "Liturgical Gestures," 6:3 (1979); "Ritual Dialogue," 7:3 (1981); "Praying the Liturgy," 11:4 (1985).

Chilson, R. *Prayer Making: Discovering the Varieties of Prayer.* Minneapolis: Winston Press, 1977.

Dietering, C. *Actions, Gestures and Bodily Attitudes.* Saratoga, CA: Resource Publications, Inc., 1980.

Fischer, B. *Signs, Words and Gestures.* New York: Pueblo, 1981.

Fleming, A. *Preparing for Liturgy.* Washington: The Pastoral Press, 1985.

Guardini, R. *Sacred Signs.* St. Louis: Pio Decimo Press, 1956.

Henderson, J. F. "Liturgical Skills." *National Bulletin on Liturgy* 17 (1984) 178–182.

Michael, C. and Norrisey, M. *Prayer and Temperament: Different Prayer Forms for Different Personality Types.* Charlottesville, VA: The Open Door, Inc., 1985.

Scarvie, W. "Liturgy and Bodiliness." *Liturgy* 16 (1971) 17–20.

Vogel, A. *Body Theology: God's Presence in Man's World.* New York: Harper and Row, 1973. Especially "Body Meaning," pp. 87–110.

Weil, L. "The Liturgy on Great Occasions: Notes on Large-Scale Celebrations." *Living Worship* 14 (1978).